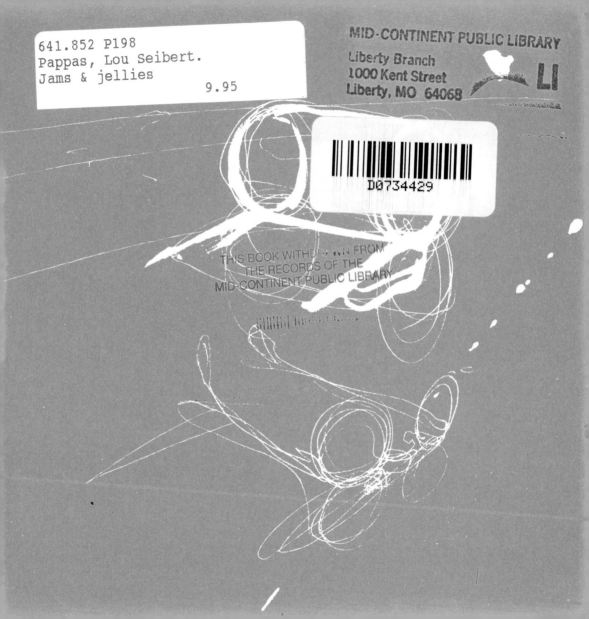

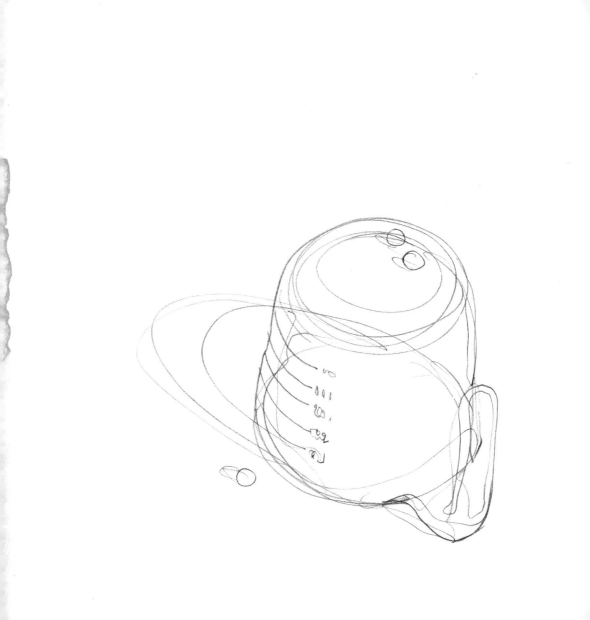

JAMS & JELLIES

LOU SEIBERT PAPPAS

ILLUSTRATIONS BY STANLEY

CHRONICLE BOOKS

SAN FRANCISCO

Library of Congress Cataloging-in-Publication Data:

Pappas, Lou Seibert.
    Jams & jellies / Lou Seibert Pappas; illustrations by Stanley.
       p.   cm.
    Includes index.
    ISBN 0-8118-1213-8
    1. Jam. 2. Jelly. 3. Fruit—Preservation.
TX612.J3P37 1996
641.8'52—dc20   95-48890
                            CIP

Printed in Hong Kong.

Book and cover design by Julia Hilgard Ritter.

Distributed in Canada by Raincoast Books
8680 Cambie Street
Vancouver, B.C. V6P 6M9

10 9 8 7 6 5 4 3 2 1

Chronicle Books
275 Fifth Street
San Francisco, CA 94103

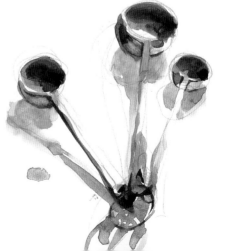

Contents

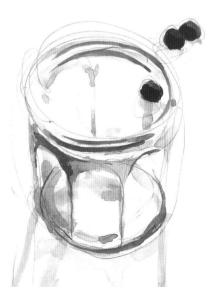

Introduction

Shimmering glasses of wild blackberry jam, huckleberry preserves, orange marmalade, strawberry jam, and raspberry-currant jelly graced the fruit cellar of my Oregon childhood home. What a treat it was to cloak homemade yeast breads—Swedish rye, four-grain, anadama, and whole-wheat loaves—with a sweet spread of intense fruit.

As a youngster, I relished our Sunday family outings picking wild berries up the Santiam River or along the Mt. Hood loop. Garnering windfall apples, Bartlett pears, Red Haven peaches, Bing cherries, and other orchard fruit from neighbors and friends was another happy pastime. Later, after my mother and I had turned the bounty into jams and jellies, I enjoyed the rewards of our efforts manyfold.

The good cooks of decades past made a production of "putting up" in quantity, often after picking the produce themselves. Over the years, as homemakers entered the workforce, this time-honored tradition was largely forgotten. My own pantry selections became limited to Santa Clara apricot jam and whole strawberry preserves made with fruit gathered from my California garden.

Today, preserving has been revolutionized. Food processors, blenders, juicers, and freezers have made this task a pleasurable, quick activity. No longer is it necessary to stock the cellar as our foremothers did. Instead, we can turn out jellies and jams on a small scale in minutes, at almost any season. Because small batches of preserves cook quicker, they are less demanding and often can be made while cooking other dishes. If you make small amounts and keep them in the refrigerator or freezer, you don't have to process them in a hot-water bath.

The microwave can be used to cook small batches of fruit, although you will need to stir frequently to keep the mixture from sticking and burning at the outer edges during the final cooking stages. It is best to work with only 1 to 2 cupfuls of fruit at a time; larger quantities take longer and tend to boil over. The microwave is best for pulpy fruit and fruit butters. Most berries and juicy fruits cook faster and better on top of the stove.

If you do choose to microwave, the container should be an ovenproof glass measure with straight sides, an open handle, and a pouring spout at least four to five times as great as the contents to be microwaved. Vented microwavable plastic wrap or an ovenproof glass lid can cover the food. Be careful to avoid steam burns by always beginning to remove the cover on the side away from you.

With the abundance of fresh, ripe fruit, including subtropical, tropical, and heirloom varieties, we are blessed with a vast number of choices, not just the staples of apples, oranges, berries, peaches, and plums. Combining two or more fruits also can create a delectable and unusual spread.

Today, our culinary horizons have broadened, and a new range of flavors is available in our kitchens. Fresh herbs, chilies, lemongrass, and ginger, among others, will add zest to our home-made preserves.

Fruit butters are quick and easy to make. It takes only minutes to puree the ingredients in a blender or food processor, then let the oven do the cooking. Some homemade fruit butters contain no sweetening or only a minimal amount of honey. Choose fruit at its peak of ripeness from your own garden, the farmer's market, U-picks, or roadside stands for the most flavorful fruit spreads.

With their superior flavor, homemade preserves are a valuable addition to any pantry and lend beauty to the table with their various hues. Because they are cheaper, fresher, low in pectin, and more flavorful, homemade preserves surpass most any that you can buy. You can also choose to make healthful and tasty preserves using organic fruits.

Jellies, jams, conserves, marmalades, and fruit butters can dress up countless snacks and lend a fillip to breads, toasts, scones, pancakes, and waffles. Some can serve as a relish or a glaze for meats or as a topping for custards, fresh or frozen yogurt, or ice cream.

Delectable preserves are a delight both to savor at home and to share as a gift for a friend or neighbor. A basket packed with three or four kinds makes a thoughtful housewarming gift or a treat at the holiday season.

I hope you will savor the easy-to-prepare jellies, jams, preserves, conserves, marmalades, and fruit butters in this book as everyday pleasures.

The Basics of Preserving

The various kinds of preserves include jellies, jams, conserves, preserves, marmalades, and fruit butters.

All preserves must have four ingredients in the proper proportion: fruit, pectin, sugar, and acid. Pectin is the fruit substance that, when heated and combined with fruit acid and sugar, makes fruit jell, or congeal. Pectin and acid vary greatly among the many kinds of fruit. Certain fruits are high in both pectin and acid; others are high in one and low in the other, or low in both. Underripe fruit often contains more pectin than does fully ripe fruit. For jelly making, it is good to select a mixture of slightly underripe and ripe fruit. A wet season with heavy rainfall produces fruit with a lower pectin content than a dry season, when the fruit will be less juicy.

In making jelly, the amount of sugar needed is determined by the pectin content of the juice. Juices rich in pectin need $3/4$ cup of sugar for each cup of juice; juices poor in pectin should have $1/2$ cup of sugar for each cup of juice. Pectin content is more important to jellies than jams, and many preserves don't need to have any added.

Juice rich in pectin may lack the acid necessary for good jelly. The fruit should be as tart as 1 teaspoon lemon juice mixed with 3 tablespoons water. If necessary, lemon juice may be added to the fruit juice. Usually 1 tablespoon lemon juice for each cup of fruit juice is sufficient.

Whenever possible, choose organic fruit, both for taste and for safety in such a concentrated product. Wash the fruit thoroughly, drain, and trim. Use a stiff brush to scrub the skin of citrus before peeling for marmalade.

Fruits high in both pectin and acid are tart apples, unripe blackberries, cranberries, currants, grapefruit, Concord and wild grapes, lemons, limes, Seville (bitter) oranges, damson plums, and unripe quinces.

Fruits high in pectin but low in acid are sweet apples, ripe blackberries, blueberries, sweet cherries, sweet oranges, semi-ripe papayas, ripe quinces, and tangerines.

Fruits high in acid and low in pectin are apricots, sour cherries, pineapple, rhubarb, and strawberries.

Fruits low in both acid and pectin are bananas, carambolas, ripe mangoes, nectarines, ripe papayas, peaches, pears, raspberries, and all overripe fruit.

A jellmeter is useful for measuring the natural pectin in fruit juice. This is a glass tube through which the extracted juice is passed; the rate of flow determines the pectin content of the juice and thus the amount of sugar to be used.

Another test for pectin content uses rubbing alcohol. *Please note: Always discard the pectin test without tasting.* Measure into a small bowl 1 teaspoon rubbing alcohol and 1 teaspoon of juice from the cooked fruit, cooled to room temperature; stir slowly and let stand for 1 minute. Juices rich in pectin will form a solid mass of gelatin, and you will need 1 cup of sugar for each cup of unsweetened juice or fruit. If large, broken flakes of gelatin form, you will need 3/4 cup of sugar for each cup of unsweetened fruit or juice. If the mixture is thin, with small gelatin flakes, the pectin is low, and you should use about 1/2 cup of sugar for each cup of juice. Another option is to concentrate the juice or fruit by boiling.

Commercial pectin is available in both liquid and powdered forms. They require a higher proportion of sugar to fruit and reduce the cooking times of jellies and jams. The two kinds of pectin are not interchangeable and each should be used as directed on the package label.

TESTING PRESERVES FOR DONENESS

There are three tests to determine whether preserves have cooked long enough to jell:

The **thermometer test** is the most accurate way of testing preserves. When a jelly or candy thermometer registers 220°F the preserves are done. For altitudes over 1,000 feet, first test the temperature of boiling water, then add 8 degrees to that figure to determine the jellying point.

The **sheet test**, or cold-spoon test, works well for jelly. Dip a cold metal spoon into the jelly, then lift it out and hold the spoon up over the mixture so that the jelly pours off the side. When the jelly slides from the side of the spoon in a sheet, rather than in separate drops, the jelly is done.

The **cold-saucer test**, or freezer test, works well for thick preserves such as jams, conserves, and marmalades. Spoon a small amount of the hot mixture onto a cold saucer and place it in the freezer for 1 minute to see if it will jell when cool.

Some preserves such as fruit butters and sun-dried tomato mixtures don't need testing and should simply be cooked until thick.

EQUIPMENT

Preserving today requires a minimum of equipment. Most of the recipes in this book will need a wide, heavy 3-, 4-, or 5-quart saucepan with a bottom surface of approximately 8 to 12 inches in diameter; a wooden spoon; measuring cups; a ladle for filling jars; a jar lifter or tongs; and a sieve or colander. A cotton jelly bag or 2 layers of cheesecloth are essential for jelly making. The jelly bag may come with a stand, or be hung from a rod or the handle of a wooden spoon so that it drips freely into a large bowl. The cheesecloth should be dampened, then squeezed dry and draped over a colander or sieve placed over a bowl. A strainer sold for making yogurt cheese is ideal. A jelly or candy thermometer is useful, and a metal rack and a big pot, such as a pasta pot, steamer, or stockpot, are necessary for sterilizing jars and hot-water processing preserves. (Allow at least 3 inches of space above the jars for processing: 1 inch for water and 2 for air space.)

In selecting the saucepan, choose heavy-gauge anodized, stainless steel, lined copper, or nonstick aluminum pans. Do not use unlined aluminum or copper, as the fruit may discolor and pick up toxic substances. A wide pan allows for quicker evaporation, which results in more flavorful preserves. The pan should be at least four times the volume of the ingredients.

Canning jars with two-part vacuum lids come in many styles, including quilted and floral jars and wide-mouthed ones. The 1/2-pint, or 8-ounce, size is ideal for most preserves as its contents can be consumed quickly and it looks attractive on the table. Use only new lids, so that they will seal properly; the metal rings may be reused if they are not dented. For refrigerator and freezer preserves, you may use the same kind of canning jar and two-part vacuum lids, or the glass-lidded French preserving jars with rubber rings and wire closures. A new rubber ring must be used each time.

STERILIZING JARS AND TWO-PART VACUUM LIDS

All jars and two-part vacuum lids must be sterilized before filling. First, wash them in hot, soapy water and rinse them. Place a rack or folded cloth in the bottom of your large pot, then fill the pot two-thirds full with hot water. Use a jar lifter or tongs to lower the jars onto the rack or cloth, tilting the jars to fill them with water so they will stand upright. Leave enough room between each jar for the water to circulate freely. Cover the jars with hot water by at least 1 inch, and leave a headspace of at least 2 inches. Cover, bring to a full, rolling boil, and adjust the heat so the water boils slowly and steadily for at least 10 minutes. Remove the jars with a jar lifter or tongs and turn them upside down on a cloth to drain.

If using two-part vacuum lids, place them in a saucepan and cover them with water. Bring the water almost to the boiling point, remove the saucepan from heat, and leave the lids and rings in the water until ready to seal the jars.

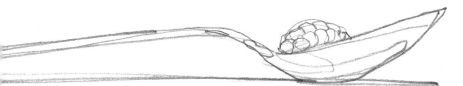

FILLING AND SEALING JARS

Fill the jars while they are still hot, leaving $1/2$ inch of headspace. Quickly remove any foam and wipe the rim of a jar with a paper towel. If using two-part vacuum lids, use tongs to remove a lid from the hot water and place it on the jar. Remove a ring from the water with tongs and set it on the jar. Using a heavy, dry cloth, screw the ring on until it is just moderately tight. Repeat to seal the remaining jars.

SHORT-TERM STORAGE

If you plan to refrigerate or freeze your preserves, they will not need to be hot-water processed and you can use either French canning jars or jars with two-part vacuum lids. For frozen preserves, use either these or freezer jars or plastic freezer containers. Let the preserves cool to room temperature, then store them in the refrigerator for up to 2 months or in the freezer for up to 1 year. The only exception is fruit butters, which have a lower sugar content; they will keep refrigerated for up to 2 to 3 weeks, or in the freezer for up to 1 year. Chest or upright freezers that maintain a 0°F temperature are preferable to the small freezer compartments of single-door refrigerators, which can range in temperature from 10° to 15°F.

HOT-WATER PROCESSING FOR LONG-TERM STORAGE

If you want to store your preserves at room temperature, you will need to process them in a hot-water bath in order to avoid spoilage. First, sterilize the jars and two-part vacuum lids as described on page 11. Fill the jars with hot preserves, allowing a $1/2$-inch headspace. Wipe the top of the jars and seal as described above. Pour all but 4 inches of water out of the large pot used for sterilizing. Using a jar lifter or tongs, carefully submerge the jars in the hot water onto the rack or cloth. When all the jars have been added, cover them with boiling water by at least 1 inch. Cover the pot and begin timing when the water reaches a boil. Adjust the heat to a low boil and process for 10 minutes for 8-ounce jars. If you are processing preserves at a high altitude, increase the processing time by 1 minute for every 1,000 feet above sea level.

Using a jar lifter or tongs, transfer the jars from the water to a towel in a draft-free place, leaving space between the jars. Let the jars cool for 12 to 24 hours, then test the seal. If the center of the lid is slightly concave, or if it pings when tapped with a teaspoon, the seal is secure. If the center of the lid is not concave, push it down with your finger. If the lid doesn't stay down, or if it makes a dull thunk when tapped, you will need to reseal and reprocess, or simply refrigerate the jar.

IMPORTANT HINTS

Select fresh seasonal fruit, preferably organic, and cook it in small batches. A small amount of fruit will cook quickly and retain its fresh taste.

Do not overcook preserves. Jams and marmalades continue to thicken after they are removed from heat. Overcooking marmalade can produce a caramelized flavor. If you are not sure whether the mixture has cooked long enough, remove it from heat, let it sit for several hours or overnight, and if it is still runny, reboil it.

PROBLEMS

Spoilage can occur if too little sugar is used, if the mixture is not cooked long enough, or if the preserves are stored in too warm a place.

Mildew can occur if cold, wet jars are used, if the preserves are stored in a damp place, or if the jars are not sealed properly.

Crystallization can occur if too much sugar is used, if the mixture is boiled before the sugar has a chance to dissolve, or if the mixture is left uncovered in the pot too long.

When jellies and preserves fail to thicken as much as desired, you have two options. You can simply return the mixture to the pot and boil it again until it tests done, or you can add 1 tablespoon of homemade or commercial pectin for each cup of preserve and then reboil the mixture until it tests done. Keep in mind that homemade jams are not as thick as the cheaper store-bought ones.

JELLIES

Jelly is made with juice and sugar. When jelled, it is clear, jewellike, and quivery. It involves two cooking processes: one to extract the juice and the second to jell the juice.

The best fruits for jelly are green apples, crab apples, blackberries, cranberries, gooseberries, grapes, plums, and lemons and oranges, particularly their peels.

For juice rich in pectin, use 3/4 cup sugar to each cup of juice. For juice low in pectin, use 1/2 cup sugar to each cup of juice. Cook small batches—4 to 6 cups of juice at a time. Bring the juice and sugar to a boil over medium heat, stirring until the sugar has dissolved, then boil rapidly until the mixture thickens and passes the thermometer test or the sheet test (see page 10).

Let the fruit drip through the jelly bag or cheesecloth at its own rate—don't squeeze the bag, or the juice will lose its clarity.

Crab Apple Jelly

This lovely pink jelly makes a delightful spread on scones or biscuits. Or use it on an open-face tea sandwich with goat cheese or natural cream cheese and garnish with a sprig of arugula or watercress.

2 pounds crab apples, quartered (about 6 cups)

3 cups water

About 2 ¼ cups sugar

3 tablespoons fresh lemon juice

Put the crab apples and water in a wide, heavy 5- or 6-quart saucepan. Cover, bring to a boil, and simmer for 20 minutes, or until the crab apples are soft. Strain the juice through a damp jelly bag or through a sieve or colander lined with 2 layers of damp cheesecloth and placed over a bowl. Measure the juice; you should have about 3 cups.

Pour the juice back into the pan and add ¾ cup sugar for each cup of juice. Add the lemon juice. Bring to a boil over medium-high heat, stirring until the sugar dissolves, and boil uncovered for 10 to 15 minutes, or until a jelly or candy thermometer registers 220°F or the mixture passes the sheet test (see page 10). Remove from heat and skim off any foam.

Ladle the jelly into hot sterilized jars and seal. Let cool, label, and refrigerate for up to 2 months, or freeze for up to 1 year. For longer storage, seal with two-part vacuum lids and process in a hot-water bath (see page 12) for 10 minutes. Let cool, label, and store in a cool, dark place.

Makes about 3 cups

Apple-Herb Jelly

Tangy apple juice makes a jelly to flavor with sage, thyme, oregano, or basil. Glaze roast chicken with a jelly made with basil; try thyme or basil with pork, and oregano with lamb roasts or chops, or in a meat sandwich spread with ricotta or cream cheese. Use sage jelly to glaze an open-face apple tart.

1 cup fresh sage, thyme, oregano, or basil
      leaves, coarsely chopped

2 1/2 cups apple juice, plus more as needed

4 cups sugar

1/4 cup fresh lemon juice or cider vinegar

One 3-ounce pouch liquid pectin

Fresh herb sprigs or leaves for garnish

Put the herbs in a small bowl. In a small saucepan, bring 1 cup of the apple juice to a boil and pour it over the herbs; cover and steep for 20 minutes. Strain and measure, adding the remaining 1 1/2 cups apple juice, plus more as needed, to make 2 1/2 cups.

Put the juice, sugar, and lemon juice or vinegar in a wide, heavy 5- or 6-quart saucepan; bring to a boil and cook over medium-high heat, stirring constantly, for about 10 minutes, or until the sugar has dissolved and the mixture reaches a rolling boil. Stir in the pectin all at once and boil hard for 1 minute, stirring constantly. Remove from heat and skim off any foam.

Place an herb sprig or leaf in each hot sterilized jelly jar, ladle in the jelly, and seal. Let cool, label, and refrigerate for up to 2 months, or freeze for up to 1 year. For longer storage, seal with two-part vacuum lids and process in a hot-water bath (see page 12) for 10 minutes. Let cool, label, and store in a cool, dark place.

Makes about 4 cups

Basic Berry Jelly

Because berries vary in their pectin content, the cooking time to reach the jelly stage may vary. The typical proportion of ingredients is ³/₄ cup sugar to 1 cup fruit juice. Let the berry juice drip naturally through the jelly bag or cheesecloth; if you squeeze or press the mixture, the jelly will not be sparkling clear.

This all-purpose recipe can be adapted for many types of fruit. A simple version for quinces follows.

1 ¹/₂ pounds blackberries, raspberries, or a mixture of currants and raspberries

About 1 ¹/₂ cups sugar

Put the berries in a wide, heavy 4- or 5-quart saucepan and crush them with a potato masher. Add just enough water to coat the bottom of the pan. Cover and cook over low heat for 5 to 10 minutes, or until the juice flows freely. Pour the juice and fruit into a damp jelly bag, or through a sieve or colander lined with 2 layers of damp cheesecloth and placed over a bowl. Let the juice flow freely for 1 to 2 hours.

Bring the juice to a boil over medium-high heat and boil uncovered for 5 minutes. Measure the juice, pour it back into the pan, and add ³/₄ cup sugar for each cup of juice. Boil the mixture uncovered again for 10 to 20 minutes, or until a jelly or candy thermometer registers 220°F or the mixture passes the sheet test (see page 10). Remove from heat and skim off any foam.

Ladle the jelly into hot sterilized jars and seal. Let cool, label, and refrigerate for up to 2 months, or freeze for up to 1 year. For longer storage, seal with two-part vacuum lids and process in a hot-water bath (see page 12) for 10 minutes. Let cool, label, and store in a cool, dark place.

Makes about 1 ¹/₂ cups

Variation To make quince jelly, follow the basic method for berry jelly. Rub the fuzz off the quinces; core, seed, and slice the fruit. Use 2 pounds of quinces and 3 cups of water to produce 2 cups of juice. Cover and simmer for 45 minutes to 1 hour to extract the juice. Use 1 cup sugar for each cup of juice.

Wine Country Rosemary Jelly

The intense flavor of rosemary infuses this burgundy-colored jelly for a delightful sandwich spread with mild goat cheese, sliced lamb or smoked turkey, and arugula or field greens. Or, use the jelly as a finishing glaze for roast lamb, beef, or duck.

1 cup fresh rosemary leaves, coarsely chopped

2 1/4 cups dry red wine such as Cabernet Sauvignon, Pinot Noir,
        or Zinfandel, plus more as needed

3 3/4 cups sugar

1/4 cup fresh lemon juice or red wine vinegar

One 3-ounce pouch liquid pectin

Fresh rosemary sprigs

Put the rosemary in a small bowl. In a small saucepan, bring 1 cup of the wine to a boil and pour it over the rosemary; cover and steep 20 minutes. Strain and measure, adding the remaining 1 1/4 cups wine, plus more as needed, to make 2 1/4 cups.

Put the wine, sugar, and lemon juice or vinegar in a wide, heavy 5- or 6-quart saucepan; bring to a boil over medium-high heat and cook, stirring constantly, for about 10 minutes, or until the sugar has dissolved. Stir in the pectin all at once and boil hard for 1 minute, stirring constantly. Remove from heat and skim off any foam.

Place an herb sprig in each hot sterilized jar, ladle in the jelly, and seal. Let cool, label, and refrigerate for up to 2 months, or freeze for up to 1 year. For longer storage, seal with two-part vacuum lids and process in a hot-water bath (see page 12) for 10 minutes. Let cool, label, and store in a cool, dark place.

Makes about 4 cups

White Wine and Herb Jelly

Aromatic herbs imbue this wine jelly with a subtlety that enhances tea sandwiches spread with ricotta or cream cheese and topped with an appropriate herb leaf or sprig.

1 cup fresh tarragon, lemon balm, or lemon geranium leaves, or dill sprigs, coarsely chopped

2 1/4 cups fruity dry white wine, such as Chablis, Gewürztraminer, or Johannisberg Riesling,
      plus more as needed

3 3/4 cups sugar

1/4 cup fresh lemon juice, white wine vinegar, or cider vinegar

One 3-ounce pouch liquid pectin

Fresh herb sprigs or leaves

Put the herbs in a small bowl. In a small saucepan, bring 1 cup of wine to a boil and pour it over the herbs; cover and steep for 20 minutes. Strain and measure, adding the remaining 1 1/4 cups wine, plus more as needed, to make 2 1/4 cups.

Put the wine, sugar, and lemon juice or vinegar in a wide, heavy 5- or 6-quart saucepan; bring to a boil over medium-high heat and cook, stirring constantly, for about 10 minutes, or until the sugar has dissolved. Stir in the pectin all at once and boil hard for 1 minute, stirring constantly. Remove from heat and skim off any foam.

Put an herb sprig or leaf in each hot sterilized jelly glass, ladle in the jelly, and seal. Let cool, label, and refrigerate for up to 2 months, or freeze for up to 1 year. For longer storage, seal with two-part vacuum lids, and process in a hot-water bath (see page 12) for 10 minutes. Let cool, label, and store in a cool, dark place.

Makes about 5 cups

Cranberry Jelly

This classic ruby jelly always accompanied the Thanksgiving bird in my childhood home in Oregon's Willamette Valley. Cranberries freeze well, so it is smart to tuck a few bags in the freezer while they are available fresh during the holiday season.

3 cups (12 ounces) cranberries

1 ¹/₂ cups water

1 ¹/₂ cups sugar

Wash and pick over the cranberries. Put them in a wide, heavy 4- or 5-quart saucepan with the water. Cover, bring to a boil, then reduce heat and simmer until the cranberries pop, about 10 minutes. Push through a sieve or a ricer with the back of a large spoon. Return to the saucepan, add the sugar, stir, and simmer uncovered until the sugar has dissolved, about 3 to 4 minutes. Then boil rapidly over medium-high heat, stirring, for 6 to 8 minutes, or until a jelly or candy thermometer registers 220°F or the mixture passes the sheet test (see page 10). Remove from heat and skim off any foam.

Ladle the jelly into hot sterilized jars and seal. Let cool, label, and refrigerate for up to 2 months, or freeze for up to 1 year. For longer storage, seal with two-part vacuum lids and process in a hot-water bath (see page 12) for 10 minutes. Let cool, label, and store in a cool, dark place.

Makes about 3 cups

Fresh Ginger Jelly

The sweet-hot flavor of this amber jelly makes a stimulating spread for cheese- and meat-topped canapes or crackers. Try it on natural cream cheese or goat cheese, topping toasted country bread, challah, or water biscuit crackers. Or lather it on a sandwich of chicken, smoked turkey, duck, or roast pork. It also enhances muffins or scones at breakfast. Select ginger that is fresh, firm, and unwrinkled. These proportions deliver a strong ginger punch—if you prefer subtlety, reduce the amount of ginger by half. The vinegar will lend a sharper tang than lemon juice.

8 ounces fresh ginger, sliced (about 2 cups)

2 cups water, plus more as needed

$^1/_3$ cup fresh lemon juice or rice wine vinegar

$3^3/_4$ cups sugar

One 3-ounce pouch liquid pectin

Combine the ginger and the 2 cups water in a blender or food processor and process until finely chopped. Pour the ginger into a fine-meshed sieve or a colander lined with 2 layers of damp cheesecloth and placed over a bowl. Let the liquid stand for 30 minutes for the sediment to settle. Pour all but the last $^1/_4$ inch into a 2-cup measure and, if necessary, add enough water to make 2 cups.

In a wide, heavy 5- or 6-quart saucepan, combine the ginger liquid, lemon juice or vinegar, and sugar; bring to a boil and cook over medium-high heat, stirring constantly, for about 10 minutes, or until the sugar has dissolved. Stir in the pectin all at once and boil hard for 1 minute, stirring constantly. Remove from heat and skim off any foam.

Ladle into hot sterilized jars and seal. Let cool, label, and refrigerate for up to 2 months, or freeze for 1 year. For longer storage, seal with two-part vacuum lids and process in a hot-water bath (see page 12) for 10 minutes. Let cool, label, and store in a cool, dark place.

Makes 4 cups

Garden Mint Jelly

Fresh mint and wine vinegar lend a refreshing tang to this shimmery jelly. Serve it on toasted white or egg bread spread with cream cheese.

1 1/2 cups packed fresh mint leaves

1 3/4 cups water, plus more as needed

1/2 cup white wine vinegar

About 3 3/4 cups sugar

One 3-ounce pouch liquid pectin

Few drops green food coloring (optional)

Chop the mint coarsely with a knife or in a food processor or blender. (Do not mince it, or the jelly will be cloudy.) Put the chopped mint in a small saucepan with the 1 3/4 cups water, bring to a boil, remove from heat, and let steep for 20 minutes. Drain through a very fine-meshed sieve, or a colander lined with 2 layers of damp cheesecloth and placed over a bowl; press lightly on the herbs with the back of a spoon to release the liquid, then discard the debris. Measure the liquid and add enough water to make 1 3/4 cups.

Pour the liquid into a wide, heavy 5- or 6-quart saucepan and stir in the vinegar and sugar. Bring to a boil over medium-high heat and cook, stirring constantly, for about 10 minutes, or until the sugar has dissolved. Add the pectin all at once and boil hard for 1 minute. Remove from heat and add a few drops of food coloring, if you like. Skim off any foam.

Ladle the jelly into hot sterilized jars and seal. Let cool, label, and refrigerate for up to 2 months, or freeze for up to 1 year. For longer storage, seal with two-part vacuum lids and process in a hot-water bath (see page 12) for 10 minutes. Let cool, label, and store in a cool, dark place.

Makes 4 cups

JAMS

Jam is made of crushed, ground, or chopped fruit cooked with sugar until thick. Use $3/4$ cup of sugar for each cup of high-pectin fruit and $1/2$ cup of sugar for each cup of low-pectin fruit. Cook until the mixture thickens and passes the thermometer test or the cold-saucer test.

Blueberry-Orange Jam

The citrus tang of lemon and orange zest enhances this deep purple blueberry jam. If you are lucky enough to find them, huckleberries are superb in this recipe.

1 pound (2 cups) blueberries or huckleberries

2 tablespoons finely julienned orange zest

1/4 cup fresh lemon juice

1 1/2 cups sugar

In a wide, heavy 3- or 4-quart saucepan, combine all the ingredients. Let stand for 1 hour for the sugar to dissolve. Bring the mixture slowly to a rapid boil over medium-high heat and cook, stirring constantly, for about 5 to 10 minutes, or until a jelly or candy thermometer registers 220°F or the mixture passes the cold-saucer test (page 10).

Ladle the jam into hot sterilized jars and seal. Let cool, label, and refrigerate for up to 2 months, or freeze for up to 1 year. For longer storage, seal with two-part vacuum lids and process in a hot-water bath (see page 12) for 10 minutes. Let cool, label, and store in a cool, dark place.

Makes about 2 cups

Raspberry-Cassis Jam

This jam is exquisite. It is wonderfully fast to make and therefore has an elegant, fresh flavor. Cassis syrup intensifies the color and flavor of the berries. Use a wide saucepan, at least 12 inches across, so the jam cooks swiftly.

4 cups fresh or frozen unsweetened raspberries

1/4 cup fresh lemon juice

3 tablespoons cassis syrup (not liqueur)

3 cups sugar

Put the berries in a wide, heavy 4- or 5-quart saucepan. Add the remaining ingredients and stir lightly. Let stand for 2 hours, stirring once or twice, or until the sugar has dissolved. Bring to a boil over medium-high heat and cook, stirring constantly, for 4 to 5 minutes or until a jelly thermometer registers 220°F or the mixture passes the cold-saucer test (see page 10). Skim off the foam.

Ladle the jam into hot sterilized jars and seal. Let cool, label, and refrigerate for up to 2 months or freeze for up to 1 year. For longer storage, seal with two-part vacuum lids and process in a hot-water bath (see page 12) for 10 minutes. Let cool, label, and store in a cool, dark place.

Makes 4 cups

Strawberry-Raspberry Refrigerator Jam

This uncooked strawberry-raspberry jam has a fresh berry flavor and a beautiful ruby color. To make a slightly less sweet sauce for drizzling over French toast, crêpes, custard, and fresh or frozen yogurt, increase the amount of crushed berries, adding an additional 1 cup strawberries and ¹/₂ cup raspberries. Store both jam and sauce in the refrigerator, or in the freezer.

6 cups strawberries, crushed (2²/₃ cups)

3 cups raspberries, crushed (1¹/₃ cups)

¹/₄ cup fresh lemon juice

One 3-ounce package powdered pectin

1 cup light corn syrup

5¹/₂ cups sugar

Put the crushed berries and lemon juice in a wide, heavy 5- or 6-quart saucepan. Slowly sift in the powdered pectin, stirring constantly. Let stand for 30 minutes, stirring occasionally. Pour in the corn syrup and mix well. Gradually stir in the sugar. Place over medium-low heat and carefully heat the mixture just to lukewarm (100°F), stirring until the sugar is dissolved.

Ladle the jam into sterilized jars or freezer containers and seal. Let cool, label, and refrigerate for up to 2 months, or freeze for up to 1 year.

Makes 8 cups

Strawberry-Rhubarb Jam

Spring strawberries and rhubarb are a complementary duo in this scarlet jam. Their peak season dovetails in springtime, so the time for combining them is brief. The slightly runny jam is nice for spooning over French toast or waffles.

8 ounces (about 2 stalks) rhubarb, thinly sliced

1 pound strawberries, hulled and sliced (about 4 cups)

2¼ cups sugar

In a wide, heavy 4- or 5-quart saucepan, layer the rhubarb and strawberries with the sugar and let stand, stirring occasionally, for 2 hours, or until the sugar has dissolved. Bring to a boil over medium-high heat and cook, stirring constantly, for 20 to 25 minutes or until a jelly or candy thermometer registers 220°F or the mixture passes the cold-saucer test (see page 10). Skim off the foam.

Ladle the jam into hot sterilized jars and seal. Let cool, label, and refrigerate for up to 2 months or freeze for up to 1 year. For longer storage, seal with two-part vacuum lids and process in a hot-water bath (see page 12) for 10 minutes. Let cool, label, and store in a cool, dark place.

Makes about 4 cups

Kiwi Fruit and Lemon Jam

With its crunchy black seeds and tangy tropical overtones, this jam is dazzling in both texture and flavor. The fruit loses its emerald green color on cooking, but the jam is luscious on open-face tea sandwiches, brioches, or toast. Because kiwi fruit is available year round, this jam can be made in any season.

1 pound (about 4 large) kiwi fruit, peeled, thinly sliced, and coarsely chopped

2 tablespoons finely julienned lemon zest

3 tablespoons fresh lemon juice

1 ½ cups sugar

Put the kiwi fruit in a wide, heavy 3- or 4-quart saucepan and sprinkle the lemon zest, lemon juice, and sugar over it. Let stand for 20 minutes, or until the sugar has dissolved. Bring to a rapid boil over medium-high heat and cook, stirring constantly, for about 15 minutes, or until a jelly or candy thermometer registers 220°F or the mixture passes the cold-saucer test (page 10).

Ladle the jam into hot sterilized jars and seal. Let cool, label, and refrigerate for up to 2 months, or freeze for up to 1 year. For longer storage, seal with two-part vacuum lids and process in a hot-water bath (see page 12) for 10 minutes. Let cool, label, and store in a cool, dark place.

Makes about 1 ½ cups

Variation *If desired, add 2 teaspoons minced lemongrass in place of the lemon zest.*

Nectarine-Amaretto Jam

Slightly unripe, firm nectarines make an even more flavorful jam than does ultra-ripe fruit. This lovely spread is ideal on an open sandwich of toasted baguette country bread spread with goat cheese.

2 pounds nectarines, pitted and cut into large pieces

2 tablespoons fresh lemon juice

3 cups sugar

$^1/_4$ cup Amaretto or brandy

In a wide, heavy 5- or 6-quart saucepan, stir together the nectarines, lemon juice, and sugar. Let stand for 1 hour, or until the sugar is dissolved. Bring to a boil over medium-high heat and cook uncovered, stirring frequently, for about 20 minutes, or until a jelly or candy thermometer registers 220°F or the mixture passes the cold-saucer test (page 10). Stir in the Amaretto or brandy and boil the jam for 1 minute, stirring constantly. Skim off the foam.

Ladle the jam into hot sterilized jars and seal. Let cool, label, and refrigerate for up to 2 months, or freeze for up to 1 year. For longer storage, seal with two-part vacuum lids and process in a hot-water bath (see page 12) for 10 minutes. Let cool, label, and store in a cool, dark place.

Makes about 4 cups

Variation *If desired, stir in $^1/_3$ cup dried cherries the last few minutes of cooking.*

Gingered Green Tomato Jam

End-of-the-season green tomatoes make an unusual preserve to pair with sharp Cheddar cheese on toasted baguette slices and serve as an appetizer. It also goes well with Gruyère or Muenster cheese and smoked turkey or Black Forest ham, for a savory sandwich on whole-grain bread or toast.

2 pounds green tomatoes

1 unpeeled lemon or lime, thinly sliced and quartered

$1/4$ cup crystallized ginger

$1/2$ cup water

3 cups sugar

In a blender or food processor, chop the tomatoes coarsely with the lemon or lime quarters and ginger. Place in a wide, heavy 5- or 6-quart saucepan, add the water, and bring to a boil over medium-high heat. Cover loosely and boil gently for about 15 minutes, or until the tomatoes and lemon or lime are tender. Let cool, cover, and let stand overnight. Bring to a rapid boil, stir in the sugar, and cook over medium-high heat, stirring constantly, for about 15 to 20 minutes, or until a jelly or candy thermometer registers 220°F or the mixture passes the cold-saucer test (page 10).

Ladle the jam into hot sterilized jars and seal. Let cool, label, and refrigerate for up to 2 months, or freeze for up to 1 year. For longer storage, seal with two-part vacuum lids and process in a hot-water bath (see page 12) for 10 minutes. Let cool, label, and store in a cool, dark place.

Makes about 3 cups

Note *This jam has a strong lemon or lime flavor. For a more mellow taste, peel the citrus zest with a vegetable peeler, then remove the white pith from the fruit and slice the fruit. Use the zest and sliced fruit in the jam.*

Hot and Sweet Red Pepper Jam

Add the chili pepper for a fiery jam, or omit it for a sweeter one. Serve this as an accompaniment to smoked turkey or as a spread for a sandwich of chicken, lamb, or Gruyère and arugula on toasted wheat or country bread.

4 large red bell peppers, halved, seeded, and deribbed

1 small fresh or dried red chili, seeded and diced (optional)

1 tablespoon kosher salt

1 1/2 cups cider vinegar

2 1/2 cups sugar

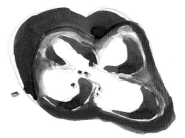

Finely chop the bell peppers and optional chili in a blender or food processor or by hand. Pour the mixture into a large bowl, sprinkle with the salt, and let stand for 30 minutes. Drain and rinse thoroughly under cold water; drain again.

Put the mixture in a wide, heavy 5- or 6-quart saucepan and add the vinegar and sugar. Bring to a boil over medium-high heat and cook, stirring occasionally, for 15 to 20 minutes, or until the peppers are translucent and a jelly or candy thermometer registers 220°F or the mixture passes the cold-saucer test (page 10).

Ladle the jam into hot sterilized jars and seal. Let cool, label, and refrigerate for up to 2 months, or freeze for up to 1 year. For longer storage, seal with two-part vacuum lids and process in a hot-water bath (see page 12) for 10 minutes. Let cool, label, and store in a cool, dark place.

Makes about 4 cups

CONSERVES AND PRESERVES

Conserves are made of two or more fruits, usually with nuts or raisins added. For best flavor and texture, add the nuts the last 1 or 2 minutes of cooking. Test for doneness with a jelly or candy thermometer or by using the cold-saucer test.

A preserve contains whole or sliced fruits cooked slowly in syrup to keep their shape. Use a jelly or candy thermometer or the cold-saucer test to see if preserves have cooked enough.

Apricot-Pistachio Conserve

Crunchy pistachios lend an appealing texture and subtle sweetness to this sprightly conserve. This is one of my favorite ways of enjoying the bounty from the two apricot trees in my garden.

1 pound apricots, pitted and coarsely chopped

1 tablespoon finely julienned lemon zest

2 tablespoons fresh lemon juice

1 ¹/₂ cups sugar

¹/₄ cup coarsely chopped pistachios

In a wide, heavy 4- or 5-quart saucepan, combine the apricots, lemon zest, lemon juice, and sugar. Let stand for 30 minutes for the sugar to dissolve. Bring to a boil over medium-high heat and cook, stirring constantly, for 15 to 20 minutes, or until a jelly or candy thermometer registers 220°F or the mixture passes the cold-saucer test (page 10). Stir in the nuts and simmer for 1 minute, stirring.

Ladle the conserve into hot sterilized jars and seal. Let cool, label, and refrigerate for up to 2 months, or freeze for up to 1 year. For longer storage, seal with two-part vacuum lids and process in a hot-water bath for 10 minutes (see page 12). Let cool, label, and store in a cool, dark place.

Makes about 2 cups

Rhubarb Conserve with Ginger and Lemon

This sophisticated conserve tingles the palate with a bright triumvirate of flavors: ginger, lemon, and rhubarb. Delightful on scones or rich biscuits, it evokes teatime in the English countryside. This is one of my favorite spreads.

1 pound (about 4 stalks) rhubarb, thinly sliced

6 tablespoons fresh lemon juice

3 tablespoons julienned lemon zest

3 cups sugar

1/4 cup crystallized ginger, finely chopped

1/3 cup almonds, toasted and coarsely chopped (see page 41)

In a wide, heavy 5- or 6-quart saucepan, combine the rhubarb, lemon juice, lemon zest, sugar, and ginger; let stand for 3 hours, or until the sugar is dissolved. Bring to a boil over medium-high heat and cook, stirring frequently, for 10 to 15 minutes, or until a jelly thermometer registers 220°F or the mixture passes the cold-saucer test (page 10). Stir in the nuts and and simmer for 1 minute, stirring.

Ladle the conserve into hot sterilized jars and seal. Let cool, label, and refrigerate for up to 2 months, or freeze for up to 1 year. For longer storage, seal with two-part vacuum lids and process in a hot-water bath (see page 12) for 10 minutes. Let cool, label, and store in a cool, dark place.

Makes about 3 1/2 cups

Peach-Pecan Conserve

The flavors of the South mingle in this luscious jam with its heady undertone of rum and brown sugar. Spread it on biscuits or scones, or use it to glaze tart shells before filling them with slightly sweetened whipped cream cheese and fresh peaches or nectarines. Or, use it to gild cream cheese tea sandwiches made with toasted brioche or challah bread.

2 pounds slightly unripe peaches or nectarines, pitted and coarsely chopped

$^1/_4$ cup fresh lemon juice

$^1/_3$ cup water

1 cup packed brown sugar

1 cup granulated sugar

$^1/_2$ cup pecans, toasted and coarsely chopped (see Note)

$^1/_4$ cup dark rum

In a wide, heavy 5- or 6-quart saucepan, combine the fruit, lemon juice, water, and brown sugar. Let stand for 1 hour, or until the brown sugar is dissolved. Bring to a boil, cover, reduce heat, and simmer for 15 minutes, or until the fruit is translucent. Add the granulated sugar, stir until dissolved, bring to a boil over medium-high heat and cook, stirring constantly, for about 15 minutes, or until a jelly or candy thermometer registers 220°F or the mixture passes the cold-saucer test (page 10). Stir in the nuts and rum and boil for 1 minute, stirring.

Ladle the conserve into hot sterilized jars and seal. Let cool, label, and refrigerate for up to 2 months, or freeze for up to 1 year. For longer storage, seal with two-part vacuum lids and process in a hot-water bath (see page 12) for 10 minutes. Let cool, label, and store in a cool, dark place.

Makes about 4 cups

Note *To toast nuts, preheat the oven to 325°F. Place the nuts in a baking pan and bake in the oven for 8 to 10 minutes, or until lightly toasted.*

Kadota Fig Conserve with Orange and Almonds

Figs lend a chewy dimension to a preserve that's ideal spread on toasted country-style bread such as ciabatta, pain levain, or pain Beaucaire. Or top the toast with a slice of Fontina and prosciutto and slather it with conserve.

2 oranges

2 pounds firm, ripe Kadota (green) figs, peeled and chopped

3 cups sugar

3 tablespoons fresh lemon juice

$^1/_2$ cup blanched almonds, toasted and coarsely chopped (page 41)

Using a potato peeler, cut the zest from the oranges and cut it into fine julienne. Peel away and discard the white pith from the oranges and dice the fruit finely. In a wide, heavy 5- or 6-quart saucepan, combine the figs, orange zest, diced oranges, sugar, and lemon juice. Let stand for 30 minutes for the sugar to dissolve.

Bring the mixture to a boil over medium-high heat and cook uncovered, stirring occasionally, for 20 to 30 minutes, or until a jelly or candy thermometer registers 220°F or the mixture passes the cold-saucer test (page 10). Stir in the nuts and simmer for 1 minute, stirring.

Ladle the conserve into hot sterilized jars and seal. Let cool, label, and refrigerate for up to 2 months, or freeze for up to 1 year. For longer storage, seal with two-part vacuum lids and process in a hot-water bath (see page 12) for 10 minutes. Let cool, label, and store in a cool, dark place.

Makes about 4 cups

Pineapple-Macadamia Conserve

With its high sugar content, pineapple makes an ultra-sweet conserve accented with lemon zest and crunchy nuts. Enjoy this as a topping on scones or biscuits, or spread on toast fingers for a tea sandwich.

2 $^{1}/_{4}$ cups diced fresh pineapple (about half a large pineapple),
      or one 20-ounce can crushedpineapple in natural juice

$^{1}/_{4}$ cup finely julienned lemon zest

3 tablespoons fresh lemon juice

1 $^{1}/_{4}$ cups sugar

$^{1}/_{4}$ cup diced macadamia nuts

In a wide, heavy 4- or 5-quart saucepan, combine the pineapple, lemon zest, lemon juice, and sugar. Let stand for 30 minutes, or until the sugar has dissolved. Bring to a boil over medium-high heat and cook, stirring constantly, for 20 to 30 minutes, or until a jelly or candy thermometer registers 220°F or the mixture passes the cold-saucer test (page 10). Stir in the nuts and and simmer for 1 minute, stirring.

Ladle the conserve into hot sterilized jars and seal. Let cool, label, and refrigerate for up to 2 months, or freeze for up to 1 year. For longer storage, seal with two-part vacuum lids and process in a hot-water bath (see page 12) for 10 minutes. Let cool, label, and store in a cool, dark place.

Makes about 1 $^{1}/_{2}$ cups

Italian Prune and Hazelnut Conserve

Toasted hazelnuts and julienned lemon zest add spark to this dark purple preserve. It is wonderful on toasted whole-grain bread. Other plum varieties in various hues can substitute for prune or purple plums.

2 pounds firm-ripe Italian prune plums or purple plums, pitted and coarsely chopped

$^1/_2$ cup water

2 tablespoons finely julienned lemon zest

3 tablespoons fresh lemon juice

3 cups sugar

$^1/_2$ cup hazelnuts, toasted, peeled, and coarsely chopped (see Note)

Put the plums in a wide, heavy 5- or 6-quart saucepan with the water, lemon zest, lemon juice, and sugar. Bring to a boil, reduce to a simmer and cook uncovered, stirring occasionally, for about 30 minutes, or until a jelly thermometer registers 220°F or the mixture passes the cold-saucer test (page 10). Stir in the nuts and and simmer for 1 minute, stirring.

Ladle the conserve into hot sterilized jars and seal. Let cool, label, and refrigerate for up to 2 months, or freeze for up to 1 year. For longer storage, seal with two-part vacuum lids and process in a hot-water bath (see page 12) for 10 minutes. Let cool, label, and store in a cool, dark place.

Makes about 4 cups

Note *To toast and peel hazelnuts, preheat the oven to 325°F. Place the nuts in a baking pan and bake in the oven for 8 to 10 minutes, or until lightly toasted. Remove from the oven and let cool for 1 minute. Then rub the nuts between two paper towels to remove the papery skins.*

Cranberry-Pistachio Conserve

This ruby-red holiday preserve is perfect with duck, venison, or smoked meats. Because it is low in sugar, it can be used as a relish.

4 cups (1 pound) cranberries

1 unpeeled orange, scrubbed, seeded, and finely chopped

1 cup sugar

$^1/_3$ cup water

3 whole cloves

One $^1/_2$-inch piece cinnamon stick

3 tablespoons Cognac or brandy

$^1/_4$ cup pistachios, coarsely chopped

Wash and pick over the cranberries; set aside. Wash, seed, and finely chop the orange. In a wide, heavy 4- or 5-quart saucepan, combine the sugar, water, chopped orange, cloves, and cinnamon, and boil for 3 minutes. Add the cranberries to the saucepan and boil over medium-high heat, stirring constantly, for about 6 minutes, or until a jelly thermometer registers 220°F or the mixture passes the cold-saucer test (page 10). Stir in the Cognac or brandy and the nuts and boil for 1 minute.

Ladle the conserve into hot sterilized jars and seal. Let cool, label, and refrigerate for up to 2 months or freeze for up to 1 year. For longer storage, seal with two-part vacuum lids and process in a hot-water bath (see page 12) for 10 minutes. Let cool, label, and store in a cool, dark place.

Makes about 3 cups

Whole Strawberry Preserve

Plump strawberries bound in a runny scarlet jelly make an intensely flavored preserve to embellish breads, waffles, oven pancakes, and even frozen yogurt or ice cream.

4 cups sugar

²/₃ cup water

4 cups strawberries, hulled

¹/₂ cup fresh lemon juice

In a wide, heavy 5- or 6-quart saucepan, combine the sugar and water, bring to a boil over medium-high heat and cook, stirring occasionally, for 5 minutes to make a thick syrup. Meanwhile, put the berries in a bowl, pour the lemon juice over them, and toss them lightly but do not crush. Add a few berries at a time to the boiling syrup, keeping the syrup boiling constantly. When all the berries are added, continue boiling, stirring occasionally, for 15 to 20 minutes, or until thick. Remove from heat, cover, and let stand for 24 hours, shaking the pan occasionally.

The next day, bring the mixture to a boil over medium-high heat and cook, stirring constantly, for 2 to 3 minutes, or until a jelly or candy thermometer registers 220°F or the mixture passes the sheet test (page 10).

Ladle the preserve into hot sterilized jars and seal. Let cool, label, and refrigerate for up to 2 months, or freeze for up to 1 year. For longer storage, seal with two-part vacuum lids and process in a hot-water bath (see page 12) for 10 minutes. Let cool, label, and store in a cool, dark place.

Makes about 4 cups

Bing Cherry Preserve with Kirsch

Bing cherries, a favorite summer fruit when I was growing up in the Northwest, are ideal for this year-round treat. Another dark-skinned cherry, the Lambert variety, can substitute; it has a softer skin and a more delicate flavor. Sour cherries also work well.

2 pounds firm, ripe Bing or Lambert sweet cherries, stemmed and pitted

3 cups sugar

¹/₄ cup fresh lemon juice

¹/₄ cup kirsch or Cherry Herring

Put the cherries in a wide, heavy 5- or 6-quart saucepan. Add the sugar and lemon juice and let stand for 1 hour, or until the sugar is dissolved. Bring the mixture to a slow boil over medium heat and cook uncovered, stirring occasionally, for about 20 minutes, or until a jelly or candy thermometer registers 220°F or the mixture passes the cold-saucer test (page 10). Stir in the kirsch or Cherry Herring.

Ladle the preserve into hot sterilized jars and seal. Let cool, label, and refrigerate for up to 2 months, or freeze for up to 1 year. For longer storage, seal with two-part vacuum lids and process in a hot-water bath (see page 12) for 10 minutes. Let cool, label, and store in a cool, dark place.

Makes 4 cups

Savory Provençal Preserve

The wonderful flavors of sunny Provence—sun-dried tomatoes, garlic, and sweet onions—mingle in this chewy preserve, which is similar to a chutney. Use it on crusty baguettes spread with goat cheese for a savory appetizer, spread it on a lamb or smoked turkey sandwich, or partner it with a lentil stew or hot specialty sausages.

1 large sweet white onion, chopped

1 yellow onion, chopped

3 garlic cloves, minced

1 cup moist-style sun-dried tomatoes, chopped (see Note)

2 tablespoons finely julienned lemon zest

$2/3$ cup sugar

$3/4$ cup water

$1/2$ cup cider vinegar

In a wide, heavy 4- or 5-quart saucepan, combine all of the ingredients. Bring to a boil, reduce heat, and simmer uncovered, stirring occasionally, for about 50 minutes, until thickened. If necessary, add more water.

Ladle the preserve into hot sterilized jars and seal. Let cool, label, and refrigerate for up to 2 months, or freeze for up to 1 year. For longer storage, seal with two-part vacuum lids and process in a hot-water bath (see page 12) for 10 minutes. Let cool, label, and store in a cool, dark place.

Makes 2 cups

Note *If the tomatoes are dry and brittle, pour hot water over them and let steep 5 minutes to soften them before chopping, then use the liquid in place of water in the recipe.*

Marmalades

Citrus fruits with their peels are the most common kind of marmalade. The peel is generally soaked or simmered in water until soft before the sugar is added. Use a jelly or candy thermometer or the cold-saucer test for marmalades. Remember that marmalade will often continue to thicken for up to 2 or 3 days after it has cooled.

Blood Orange Marmalade

A lovely rosy-orange hue identifies this tangy marmalade made from blood oranges. Plan to make it over a 2-day time span, as the peel needs to thoroughly soften by soaking for at least 12 hours.

5 blood oranges, scrubbed well and halved

About 1 1/2 cups water

About 1 3/4 cups sugar

Squeeze the juice from the oranges. Cut the peel into very fine julienne. Combine the juice and peel (you should have about 2 1/2 cups) in a wide, heavy 5- or 6-quart saucepan. Add 1 1/2 cups water, or enough to make the mixture slushy. Cover and let soak 12 hours or overnight.

Bring the mixture to a boil, reduce heat, cover, and simmer for 10 minutes. Remove from heat and measure the mixture, then return it to the pan. Add 3/4 cup sugar for each cup of fruit and liquid. Let stand for 30 minutes, stirring once or twice. Bring to a rapid boil over medium-high heat and cook, stirring constantly, for 15 to 20 minutes, or until a jelly or candy thermometer registers 220°F or the mixture passes the cold-saucer test (see page 10).

Ladle the marmalade into hot sterilized jars and seal. Let cool, label, and refrigerate for up to 2 months, or freeze for up to 1 year. For longer storage, seal with two-part vacuum lids and process in a hot-water bath (see page 12) for 10 minutes. Let cool, label, and store in a cool, dark place.

Makes 2 cups

Mango-Orange Marmalade with Honey

Mangoes make a delectable spread when lightly sweetened with honey. Parboiling the julienned citrus peel tenderizes it and removes the bitterness, but this step is not essential. This marmalade is delicious on hot breads. Or, blend the marmalade with a spoonful of Dijon mustard and a squeeze of lemon juice to use as a coating for roast chicken breasts or pork loin.

Zest of 1 orange, cut into fine julienne

Zest of 1 lemon, cut into fine julienne

2 large mangoes, peeled, cut from the pit, and diced (2 cups)

3 tablespoons fresh lemon juice

$1/2$ cup orange juice

$1/2$ cup sugar

$1/4$ cup honey

Place the orange and lemon zest in a small saucepan, cover with water, and simmer for 5 minutes, or until soft; drain. Place the diced mangoes in a wide, heavy 4- or 5-quart saucepan and add the lemon juice, orange juice, orange and lemon zest, and sugar. Let stand for 1 hour, or until the sugar is dissolved. Bring to a boil over medium-high heat and cook, stirring frequently, for 10 minutes. Add the honey and cook for 2 minutes, or until thickened.

Ladle into hot sterilized jars and seal. Let cool, label, and refrigerate for up to 2 months, or freeze for up to 1 year. For longer storage, seal with two-part vacuum lids and process in a hot-water bath (see page 12) for 10 minutes. Let cool, label, and store in a cool, dark place.

Makes 2 cups

Mom's Orange Marmalade

Navel oranges from my garden produce the kind of chewy marmalade that was a childhood favorite. My preference is for long, slightly thick strands of peel, but if you like a finer texture, slice the peel into fine julienne.

5 large navel oranges, scrubbed and peeled

3/4 cup fresh lemon juice

About 5 cups sugar

Put the orange peel in a wide, heavy 5- or 6-quart saucepan and add water to cover. Bring to a boil, reduce heat, cover, and simmer, for 20 minutes. Lift out the peel with a slotted spoon and reserve the water. Let the peel cool to the touch. Using a curved serrated knife or a spoon, remove the stringy white part but don't make the peel too thin. Cut the peel into julienne. Remove any strings from the peeled oranges and cut the oranges into very thin crosswise slices.

Put the orange slices and peel in a wide, heavy 5- or 6-quart saucepan and pour in the water reserved from cooking the peel. Add the lemon juice. Let stand for 30 minutes. Cover and simmer for 20 to 25 minutes, or until the peel is soft.

Measure the mixture, return it to the pan, and add 3/4 cup of sugar for each cup of fruit and liquid. Stir well and let sit for 1 hour, or until the sugar is dissolved. Bring to a boil and cook over medium-high heat, stirring constantly, for about 15 minutes, or until a jelly or candy thermometer registers 220°F or the mixture passes the cold-saucer test (page 10).

Ladle the marmalade into hot sterilized jars and seal. Let cool, label, and refrigerate for up to 2 months, or freeze for up to 1 year. For longer storage, seal with two-part vacuum lids and process in a hot-water bath (see page 12) for 10 minutes. Let cool, label, and store in a cool, dark place.

Makes about 6 cups

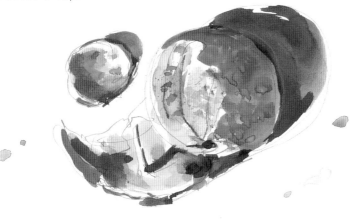

Three-Citrus Marmalade

Choose pale yellow grapefruit for this marmalade so the colors will blend nicely. Once preserved, the three citrus peels make a fascinating intermingling of distinctive tastes.

1 small grapefruit

1 large orange

1 lemon

About 4 cups water

About 4 cups sugar

Scrub and peel the grapefruit, orange, and lemon. Put the peel in a wide, heavy 5- or 6-quart saucepan and add water to barely cover. Bring to a boil, reduce heat, cover, and simmer, for 10 minutes; drain. Add fresh water to barely cover and boil for 10 minutes. Remove the peel with a slotted spoon and reserve the water. Let the peel cool, then cut it into fine julienne. Thinly slice the fruit crosswise and cut it into small pieces. Return the fruit, peel, and reserved water to the saucepan, bring to a boil, reduce heat, and simmer for 30 minutes. Let cool.

Measure the mixture, return it to the saucepan, and for every cup of fruit and juice add ³/₄ cup of sugar. Bring to a boil over medium-high heat and cook, stirring constantly, for about 20 minutes, or until a jelly or candy thermometer registers 220°F or the mixture passes the cold-saucer test (page 10).

Ladle the marmalade into hot sterilized jars and seal. Let cool, label, and refrigerate for up to 2 months, or freeze for up to 1 year. For longer storage, seal with two-part vacuum lids and process in a hot-water bath (see page 12) for 10 minutes. Let cool, label, and store in a cool, dark place.

Makes about 5 cups

Chili-Lime Marmalade

This spicy, hot-sweet spread goes well with grilled or roast pork or duck. Or pair it with natural cream cheese and water biscuits for an appetizer. Plan to make it over a 2-day time span, as the fruit and chili need to soak for 12 hours.

3 large limes

1 lemon

1 small jalapeño chili, seeded and minced

About 2 cups water

About 2 1/4 cups sugar

Slice the limes and lemon very thinly crosswise and quarter the slices. Place the fruit and chili in a wide, heavy 4- or 5-quart saucepan, add enough of the water to barely cover, and let soak for 12 hours. Bring to a boil, reduce heat, cover, and simmer, stirring occasionally, for about 20 minutes, or until the peel is tender and translucent. Measure this mixture and return it to the pan. Add 1 cup sugar for every cup of the mixture. Bring to a boil over medium-high heat and cook uncovered, stirring occasionally, for about 20 minutes, or until a jelly thermometer registers 220°F or the mixture passes the cold-saucer test (page 10).

Ladle the marmalade into hot sterilized jars and seal. Let cool, label, and refrigerate for up to 2 months, or freeze for up to 1 year. For longer storage, seal with two-part vacuum lids and process in a hot-water bath (see page 12) for 10 minutes. Let cool, label, and store in a cool, dark place.

Makes about 3 cups

Ruby Red Grapefruit Marmalade

Ruby red grapefruit produce a pretty rosy pink marmalade strewn with threads of tender golden peel.

2 large ruby red grapefruit, scrubbed and peeled

3 tablespoons fresh lemon juice

About 1 1/2 cups water

About 4 1/2 cups sugar

Put the grapefruit peel in a wide, heavy 5- or 6-quart saucepan and cover with water. Bring to a boil, reduce heat, cover, and simmer for 5 minutes. Drain. Add fresh water to cover, boil another 5 minutes, and drain again. Repeat for a third time and drain. Using a curved serrated knife or a spoon, remove any stringy white part from the peel but don't make the peel too thin. Cut the peel into fine julienne. Remove any pith from the peeled grapefruit, slice the fruit very thinly crosswise, and cut it into small pieces.

Put the fruit, peel, and lemon juice in the same saucepan. Add water just to cover, about 1 1/2 cups. Bring to a boil, reduce heat, and simmer uncovered for 30 minutes, or until the peel is very tender. Measure the mixture and return it to the saucepan. Add 1 cup sugar for each cup of the mixture. Bring to a boil over medium-high heat and cook uncovered, stirring occasionally, for about 20 minutes, or until a jelly or candy thermometer registers 220°F or the mixture passes the cold-saucer test (page 10), about 20 minutes.

Ladle the marmalade into hot sterilized jars and seal. Let cool, label, and refrigerate for up to 2 months, or freeze for up to 1 year. For longer storage, seal with two-part vacuum lids and process in a hot-water bath (see page 12) for 10 minutes. Let cool, label, and store in a cool, dark place.

Makes about 4 1/2 cups

59

FRUIT BUTTERS

Fruit that has been pureed, blended, or pushed through a sieve or colander and cooked until thick enough to spread is called a fruit butter. Although fruit butters can be made with no sugar or with considerably less than is used for jams and jellies, they cannot be refrigerated as long as other preserves; they will keep in the refrigerator for up to 2 or 3 weeks.

Sugar-Free Apple Butter

This easy spread bakes to a caramelized hue. Various apple varieties will lend different flavors, varying from sweet to tart, so wait and add a touch of spice at the end of cooking.

2 pounds Granny Smith, Winesap, pippin, or other tart apples,
        peeled, cored, and coarsely chopped
1 can (6 ounces) thawed frozen apple juice concentrate
Ground cinnamon or mace to taste

Preheat the oven to 300°F. Puree the apples, in batches if necessary, in a blender or food processor with the thawed apple concentrate. Place the mixture in a glass or ceramic baking dish, season with cinnamon or mace, and bake, stirring 2 or 3 times, for 1 hour, or until golden brown and reduced by half.

Ladle the apple butter into hot sterilized jars and seal. Let cool, label, and refrigerate for up to 2 weeks or freeze for up to 1 year. For longer storage, seal with two-part vacuum lids and process in a hot-water bath (see page 12) for 10 minutes. Let cool, label, and store in a cool, dark place.

Makes about 2 cups

Orange-Apricot Butter with Honey

The sweet-tart intensity of apricots comes through in this thick spread accented with orange zest and honey. It makes a lovely topping for toast, or spread it on crepes or Belgian waffles. It's also good on nut bread for a quick snack or tea treat, or you can stir a spoonful into plain yogurt for a fast snack. This is the recipe for those extra-ripe apricots if you have them. Choose a honey with a strong fragrance and flavor, such as wildflower or eucalyptus.

1 orange

2 pounds apricots, pitted and coarsely chopped

3 tablespoons strong-flavored honey

Preheat the oven to 300°F. Use a potato peeler to remove the orange zest. Cut it into fine julienne. In a blender or food processor, puree the orange zest with the apricots and honey until smooth. Pour into a glass or ceramic baking dish and bake, stirring 2 or 3 times, for 1 hour, or until thickened.

Ladle the butter into hot sterilized jars and seal. Let cool, label, and refrigerate for up to 2 weeks, or freeze for up to 1 year. For longer storage, seal with two-part vacuum lids and process in a hot-water bath (see page 12) for 10 minutes. Let cool, label, and store in a cool, dark place.

Makes about 4 cups

Orange-Pear Butter with Ginger

Orange zest and ginger perfume this honey-sweetened spread with an intriguing granular texture. Scones, muffins, and brioche loaves are natural companions for it.

2 pounds Anjou or Bartlett pears, peeled, cored, and coarsely chopped

2 tablespoons honey

4 orange zest strips, cut into fine julienne

$^1/_4$ cup crystallized ginger, thinly sliced

Ground mace to taste

Preheat the oven to 300°F. Puree the pears in a blender or food processor with the honey, orange zest, ginger, and mace. Place in a glass or ceramic baking dish and bake, stirring 2 or 3 times, for 1 hour, or until reduced by half and a light golden brown.

Ladle the butter into hot sterilized jars and seal. Let cool, label, and refrigerate for up to 2 weeks, or freeze for up to 1 year. For longer storage, seal with two-part vacuum lids and process in a hot-water bath (see page 12) for 10 minutes. Let cool, label, and store in a cool, dark place.

Makes about 2 cups

Plum Butter with Orange and Honey

Add honey to taste to this refreshing butter, as plums can vary in sweetness.

2 pounds Satsuma or other plums, pitted and coarsely chopped

2 to 4 tablespoons orange blossom or other mild-flavored honey

6 orange zest strips, cut into fine julienne

Ground nutmeg to taste

Preheat the oven to 300°F. Puree the plums in a blender or food processor with the honey, orange zest, and nutmeg. Place in a glass or ceramic baking dish and bake, stirring 2 or 3 times, for 1 hour, or until reduced by half and thickened.

Ladle the butter into hot sterilized jars and seal. Let cool, label, and refrigerate for up to 2 weeks, or freeze for up to 1 year. For longer storage, seal with two-part vacuum lids and process in a hot-water bath (see page 12) for 10 minutes. Let cool, label, and store in a cool, dark place.

Makes about 2 cups

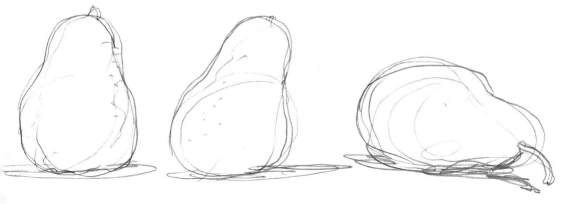

Mango Butter with Ginger and Lime

Crystallized ginger and lime juice heighten the flavor of this golden spread. It particularly enhances toasted English muffins, scones, and pecan or macadamia nut waffles or pancakes.

2 large mangoes (about 3 pounds), peeled, cut from the pit, and coarsely chopped

2 tablespoons honey

$^1/_3$ cup fresh lime juice

$^1/_3$ cup crystallized ginger, thinly sliced

Ground nutmeg to taste (optional)

Preheat the oven to 300°F. Puree the mangoes in a blender or food processor with the honey, lime juice, and crystallized ginger. Place in a glass or ceramic baking dish and bake, stirring 2 or 3 times, for 1 to 1$^1/_4$ hours, or until reduced by half and thickened. If desired, season with nutmeg.

Ladle the butter into hot sterilized jars and seal. Let cool, label, and refrigerate for up to 2 weeks, or freeze for up to 1 year. For longer storage, seal with two-part vacuum lids and process in a hot-water bath (see page 12) for 10 minutes. Let cool, label, and store in a cool, dark place.

Makes about 3 cups

Papaya and Passion Fruit Butter

This pretty golden orange spread is an exotic flavor blend of three fruits: papaya, passion fruit, and orange. It takes just minutes to prepare. Passion fruit vinegar, made by the Napa Valley Kitchens, is available in gourmet shops.

1 large papaya (about 1 1/2 pounds), peeled, seeded, and coarsely chopped

1/4 cup passion fruit vinegar or fresh lime juice

1/4 cup thawed frozen orange juice concentrate

3 to 4 tablespoons honey

Preheat the oven to 300°F. Puree the papaya in a blender or food processor with the vinegar or lime juice, orange juice, and honey to taste. Place in a glass or ceramic baking dish and bake, stirring 2 or 3 times, for 1 to 1 1/4 hours, or until reduced by half and thickened.

Ladle the butter into hot sterilized jars and seal. Let cool, label, and refrigerate for up to 2 weeks, or freeze for up to 1 year. For longer storage, seal with two-part vacuum lids and process in a hot-water bath (se~ page 12) for 10 minutes. Let cool, label, and store in a cool, dark p'

Makes about 1 1/2 cups

Berry Syrup

This exquisite fruit syrup is a wonderful flavoring. Blend it into a milk shake or ice cream soda, or use it as a sauce for vanilla frozen yogurt or plain yogurt topped with muesli or granola.

4 cups raspberries, blackberries, hulled strawberries, Loganberries, or Marionberries

1 cup water

About 2 cups sugar

Place the fruit in a wide, heavy 4- or 5-quart saucepan, add the water, and bring to a boil. Reduce the heat and simmer gently for 10 minutes, uncovered. Strain through a damp jelly bag or through a sieve or colander lined with 2 layers of damp cheesecloth and placed over a bowl, pressing the fruit lightly with the back of a large spoon. Measure the juice and return the juice to the saucepan. Add 1 cup sugar for each cup of juice. Bring to a boil over medium-high heat and cook uncovered, stirring occasionally, for 2 to 3 minutes, or until slightly thickened.

Pour the syrup into hot sterilized jars or bottles and seal. Let cool, label, and refrigerate for up to 2 months, or freeze for up to 1 year. For longer storage, seal with two-part vacuum lids and process in a hot-water bath (see page 12) for 10 minutes. Let cool, label, and store in a cool, dark place.

Makes about 2 cups

Whipped Honey Butter

Though not really a preserve, this spread is an ideal topping for muffins, scones, biscuits, French toast, and waffles. Light and fluffy, it melts into a smooth, delicious pool. Select a strong-flavored honey for the most flavor.

³/4 cup strong-flavored honey, such as wildflower

¹/2 cup butter at room temperature

Place the honey in the bowl of an electric mixer and beat with the wire whip attachment (or beat with a hand-held mixer) until it turns white and fluffy, about 5 minutes. Gradually beat in the butter until blended. Turn into a bowl or jar, cover, and refrigerate for up to 2 weeks.

Makes about 2 cups

Index

Table of Equivalents

The exact equivalents in the following tables have been rounded for convenience.

US/UK

oz=ounce

lb=pound

in=inch

ft=foot

tbl=tablespoon

fl oz=fluid ounce

qt=quart

METRIC

g=gram

kg=kilogram

mm=millimeter

cm=centimeter

ml=milliliter

l=liter

OVEN TEMPERATURES

Fahrenheit	Celsius	Gas
250	120	1/2
275	140	1
300	150	2
325	160	3
350	180	4
375	190	5
400	200	6
425	220	7
450	230	8
475	240	9
500	260	10

WEIGHTS

US/UK	Metric
1 oz	30 g
2 oz	60 g
3 oz	90 g
4 oz (1/4 lb)	125 g
5 oz (1/3 lb)	155 g
6 oz	185 g
7 oz	220 g
8 oz (1/2 lb)	250 g
10 oz	315 g
12 oz (3/4 lb)	375 g
14 oz	440 g
16 oz (1 lb)	500 g
1 1/2 lb	750 g
2 lb	1 kg
3 lb	1.5 kg

LIQUIDS

US	Metric	UK
2 tbl	30 ml	1 fl oz
1/4 cup	60 ml	2 fl oz
1/3 cup	80 ml	3 fl oz
1/2 cup	125 ml	4 fl oz
2/3 cup	160 ml	5 fl oz
3/4 cup	180 ml	6 fl oz
1 cup	250 ml	8 fl oz
1 1/2 cups	375 ml	12 fl oz
2 cups	500 ml	16 fl oz
4 cups/1 qt	1 l	32 fl oz

LENGTH MEASURES

US/UK	Metric
1/8 in	3 mm
1/4 in	6 mm
1/2 in	12 mm
1 in	2.5 cm
2 in	5 cm
3 in	7.5 cm
4 in	10 cm
5 in	13 cm
6 in	15 cm
7 in	18 cm
8 in	20 cm
9 in	23 cm
10 in	25 cm
11 in	28 cm
12 in/1 ft	30 cm

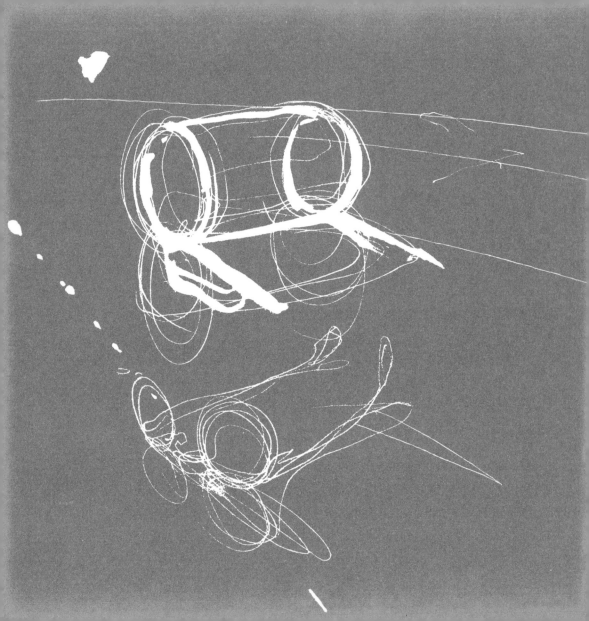